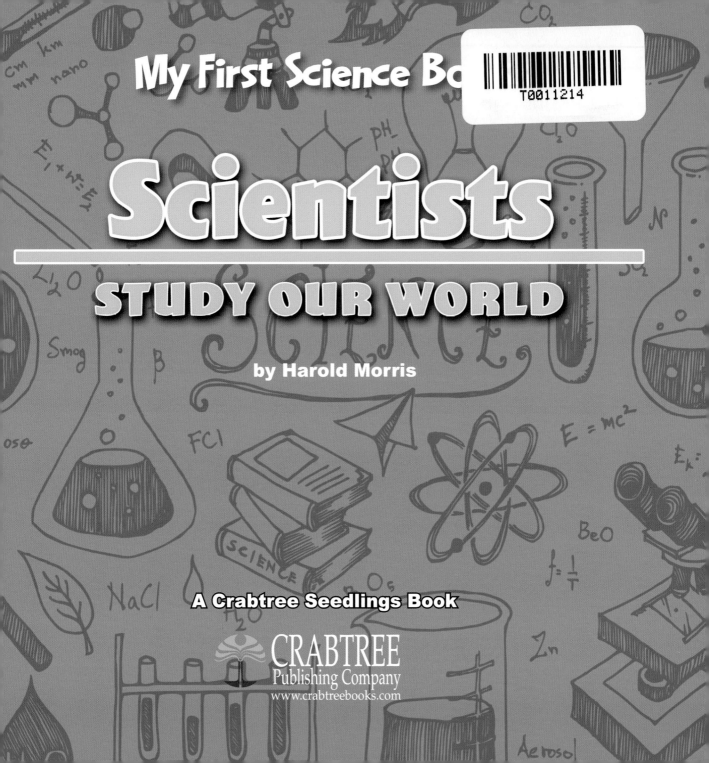

My First Science Book

Scientists

STUDY OUR WORLD

by Harold Morris

A Crabtree Seedlings Book

CRABTREE
Publishing Company
www.crabtreebooks.com

T0011214

School-to-Home Support for Caregivers and Teachers

This book helps children grow by letting them practice reading. Here are a few guiding questions to help the reader with building his or her comprehension skills. Possible answers appear here in red.

Before Reading:

• What do I think this book is about?
- *I think this book is about scientists.*
- *I think this book is about our world.*

• What do I want to learn about this topic?
- *I want to learn if it's hard to become a scientist.*
- *I want to learn more about planet Earth.*

During Reading:

• I wonder why...
- *I wonder why there are so many different kinds of scientists.*
- *I wonder why you have to go to school to become a scientist.*

• What have I learned so far?
- *I have learned that geology is the study of our Earth and what it is made of.*
- *I have learned that Earth is over 4 billion years old.*

After Reading:

• What details did I learn about this topic?
- *I have learned that dinosaurs lived on Earth about 180 million years ago.*
- *I have learned that a meteorologist studies the weather.*

• Read the book again and look for the vocabulary words.
- *I see the word **observing** on page 2, and the word **endangered** on page 8.*

Table of Contents

What Do Scientists Do?

Scientists study our world. Like scientists, we can learn about our world by **observing** and experimenting.

DICTIONARY
A-Z

observing (uhb-ZERV-ing): noticing by watching carefully

Let's find out more about science and scientists!

Biology (bye-OL-uh-jee):

Biology is the **scientific** study of ALL living things.

Thanks to biologists, we know a lot about people, plants, and animals.

scientific (SYE-uhn-ti-fik): based on science

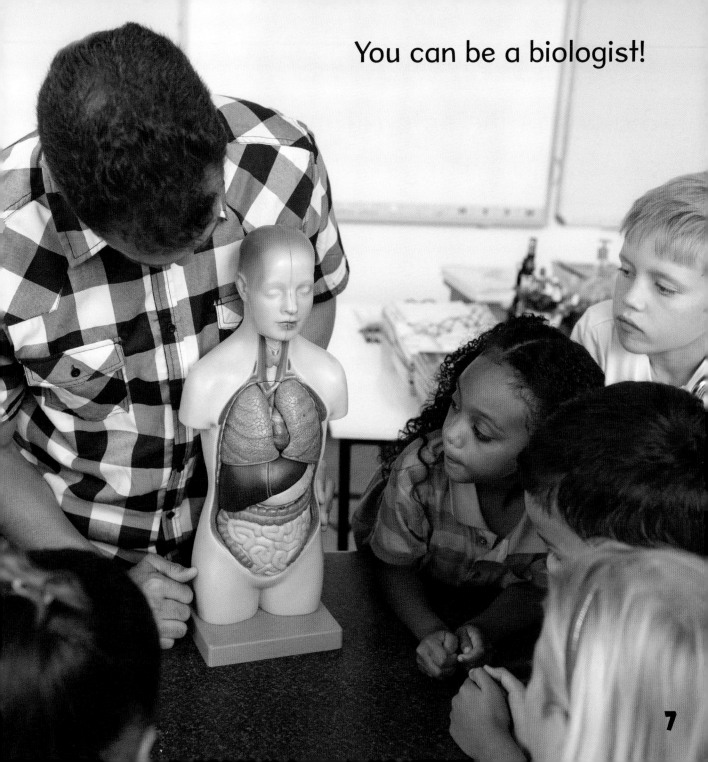

You can be a biologist!

Chemistry (KEM-is-tree):

Chemistry is the scientific study of **substances**. Chemists study what substances are made of and how they react with each other.

Thanks to chemists, we have life-saving medicines, such as penicillin.

substances (SUHB-stuhnss-iz): powders, liquids, and solid objects

DICTIONARY A-Z

You can be a chemist!

Oceanography (oh-shuh-NOG-ruh-fee):

Oceanography is the science that deals with the oceans, and the plants and animals that live in them.

Thanks to oceanographers, we know which ocean plants and animals are **endangered** and how to help them.

endangered (en-DAYN-jurd): plant or animal species in danger of having no living members

DICTIONARY
A-Z

You can be an oceanographer!

Astronomy (uh-STRON-uh-mee):

Astronomy is the scientific study of stars, planets, and space.

Thanks to astronomers, we now know that there are eight planets in our solar system, and billions of solar systems in the universe.

You can be an astronomer!

Botany (BOT-uh-nee):

Botany is the scientific study of plants. It is also called *plant biology*.

Thanks to botanists, we know plants use **photosynthesis** to make their own food.

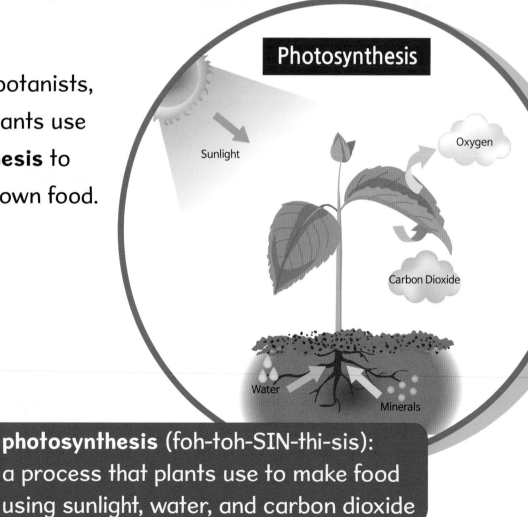

Photosynthesis

Sunlight

Oxygen

Carbon Dioxide

Water

Minerals

DICTIONARY

photosynthesis (foh-toh-SIN-thi-sis): a process that plants use to make food using sunlight, water, and carbon dioxide

You can be a botanist!

Geology (jee-OL-uh-jee):

Geology is the scientific study of our Earth, to learn what it is made of and how it works.

Thanks to geologists studying and testing rocks, we know that Earth is over 4 billion years old!

You can be
a geologist!

Paleontology (pale-ee-uhn-TOL-uh-jee):

Paleontology is the science that deals with fossils and other **ancient** life-forms.

Thanks to paleontologists, we know dinosaurs lived on Earth for about 180 million years.

DICTIONARY

ancient (AYN-shunt): belonging to a time long ago, in this case *prehistoric* time

You can be a
paleontologist!

Meteorology (mee-tee-uh-ROL-uh-jee)

Meteorology is the study of Earth's **atmosphere**, climate, and weather.

Thanks to meteorologists, we know the daily temperature and when a dangerous storm is coming.

DICTIONARY **atmosphere** (AT-muhs-fihr): the layer of gases that surrounds a planet

You can be a
meteorologist!

Ecology (ee-KOL-uh-jee)

Ecology is the study of the relationship between plants, animals, and their **environment**.

Thanks to ecologists, we understand how to better take care of our Earth.

DICTIONARY **environment** (en-VYE-ruhn-muhnt): the natural world of the land, sea, and air

You can be an ecologist!

INDEX

Written by: Harold Morris

Print coordinator: Katherine Berti

PHOTO CREDITS:

COVER: istock.com | LightField Studios, illustrations by veekicl istock. com. Page 2-3: istock.com | ajr_images. Page 4-5: istock.com | shironosov, shutterstock.com | Ilike. Page 6-7: shutterstock.com | pixelrain, shutterstock.com | wavebreakmedia. Page 8-9: istock.com | scanrail, shutterstock.com | Elena Nichizhenova. Page 10-11: shutterstock.com | Nicole Helgason, istock.com | Bicho_raro. Page 12-13: istock.com | Stolk, shutterstock.com | AlohaHawaii. Page 14-15: shutterstock.com | Jakinnboaz, istock.com |romrodinka. Page 116-17: istock.com | buranatrakul, istock.com | robertprzybysz. Page 18-19: shutterstock.com | ermess, shutterstock.com | all_about_people. Page 20-21: shutterstock.com | Rawpixel.com, Michael Gray | Dreamstime.com. Page 22-23: istock.com | Highwaystarz-Photography, istock.com | tatyana_tomsickova.

Library and Archives Canada Cataloguing in Publication

Title: Scientists study our world / by Harold Morris.
Names: Morris, Harold, author.
Description: Series statement: My first science books | "A Crabtree seedlings book". | Includes index.
Identifiers: Canadiana (print) 20210203919 |
    Canadiana (ebook) 20210203927 |
    ISBN 9781427159519 (hardcover) |
    ISBN 9781427159489 (softcover) |
    ISBN 9781427160164 (HTML) |
    ISBN 9781427160133 (EPUB) |
    ISBN 9781427160218 (read-along ebook)
Subjects: LCSH: Science—Vocational guidance—Juvenile literature. |
    LCSH: Scientists—Juvenile literature.
Classification: LCC Q147 .M67 2022 | DDC j502.3—dc23

Library of Congress Cataloging-in-Publication Data

Available at the Library of Congress

Crabtree Publishing Company

www.crabtreebooks.com   1-800-387-7650

Print book version produced jointly with Blue Door Education 2022

Printed in the U.S.A./062021/CG20210401

Published in the United States
Crabtree Publishing
347 Fifth Avenue, Suite 1402-145
New York, NY, 10016

Published in Canada
Crabtree Publishing
616 Welland Ave.
St. Catharines, Ontario L2M 5V6